Level Four
D/Grade 2½

John W. Schaum

Interval Speller

for Piano, Electronic Keyboard or Organ

FOREWORD

The aim of this book is to provide the student with a thorough understanding of all the major, minor, perfect, augmented and diminished intervals. This knowledge will equip the pupil with the necessary background for harmonic analysis and chord construction.

All lessons are also to be performed at the keyboard so that the sound of each interval is recognized.

To facilitate the correcting of the assignments, an answer page is supplied on page 23. It is recommended that the answer page be removed before the student starts the book.

Progressive Succession of Schaum Workbooks:

Title	Level
Theory Workbook, Level Two	B/Grade 1½
Rhythm Workbook, Level Two	B/Grade 1½
Easy Keyboard Harmony, Book 1 (Level Two)	B/Grade 1½
Scale Speller (Level Two)	B/Grade 1½
Theory Workbook, Level Three	C/Grade 2
Rhythm Workbook, Level Three	C/Grade 2
Easy Keyboard Harmony, Book 2 (Level Three)	C/Grade 2
Arpeggio Speller (Level Three)	C/Grade 2
Easy Keyboard Harmony, Book 3 (Level Four)	D/Grade 2½
Interval Speller (Level Four)	D/Grade 2½
Easy Keyboard Harmony, Book 4 (Level Five)	E/Grade 3
Chord Speller (Level Five)	E/Grade 3
Easy Keyboard Harmony, Book 5 (Level Six)	F/Grade 4

SCHAUM PUBLICATIONS, INC.
10235 N. Port Washington Rd. - Mequon, WI 53092

02-50
BL-19

CONTENTS

Music to Correlate with the Level Four Curriculum (D/Grade 2½)

Method: Making Music at the Piano, Level 4 (basic)
Piano for Adults, Level 4 (adult)
Easy Keyboard Harmony, Bk. 3 (improvising)

Technic: Fingerpower, Level 4

Theory: Theory Workbook, Level 4

Repertoire:

Best of Bach	Best of Tchaikowsky	Hymns & Gospel Songs
Best of Beethoven	Christmas Carols & Hymns	Nutcracker Suite
Best of Mozart	Christmas Songs & Tunes	Repertoire Highlights, Level 4
Best of Schubert	Easy Master Themes, Level 4	Rhythm & Blues, Bk. 3

Lesson 1. Interval Number Names

Teacher's Note: It is recommended that the answer page on page 23 be removed before the student starts the book.

Pupil's Name.................................... Completion Date....................................

Assignment Date.................................... Grade or Star....................................

An INTERVAL is the distance between two tones. Intervals are named by their numerical size. From C to D is a SECOND, because it includes TWO letters: C and D. From C to E is a THIRD (comprising THREE letters: C, D, E). Similarly from C to F is a FOURTH; from C to G is a FIFTH; etc. The number name is NOT affected by accidental signs (♯, ♭, or ♮). For example, each of the following intervals is a FIFTH:

DIRECTIONS: Write the number name for each of the following intervals. The number name is determined by counting the alphabetical (staff) degrees from the lower to the upper tone, both included. Study the samples.

Samples

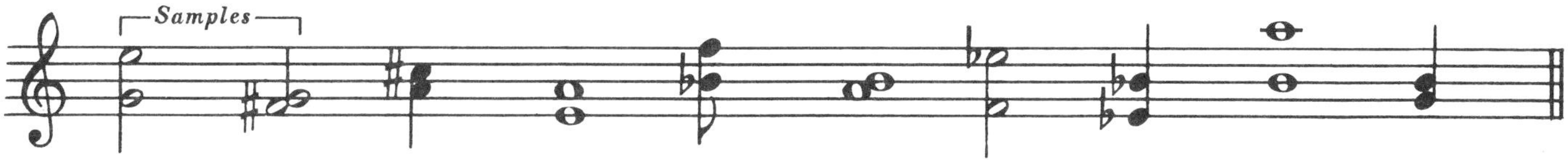

6 2

(Write number names)

(Write number names)

(Write number names)

(Write number names)

(Write number names)

(Write number names)

Teacher's Note: The purpose of this lesson is to learn the number names of the intervals. The harmonic explanation of the different types of intervals will be presented later in the book.

Lesson 2. Building Intervals

Pupil's Name.. *Completion Date*..

Assignment Date.. *Grade or Star*..

Intervals may be sounded simultaneously or in succession. HARMONIC intervals are sounded simultaneously. See Ex.1. MELODIC intervals are sounded in succession as in Ex.2.

Ex.1  Ex.2 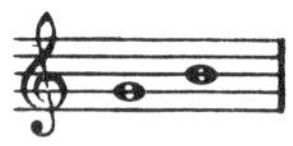

From an analytical standpoint both the above types of intervals are identical. For purposes of clarity, the Schaum Interval Speller will present intervals exclusively in their harmonic form. On the staffs below, write harmonic intervals. Follow this procedure on all succeeding assignments.

Write a whole note a SECOND above each of the following notes.

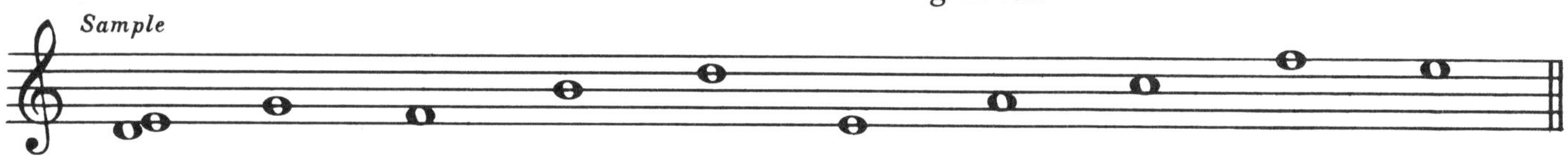

Write a whole note a THIRD above each of the following notes.

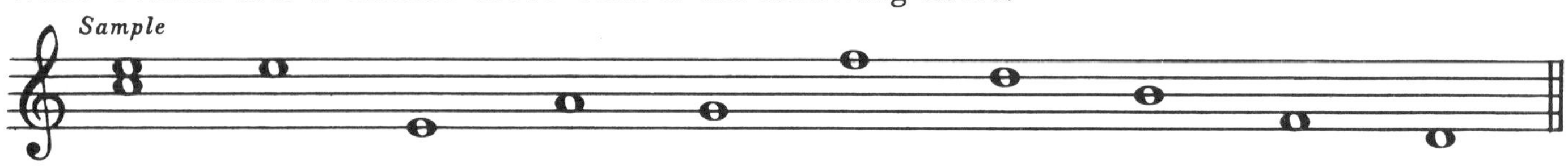

Write a whole note a FOURTH above each of the following notes.

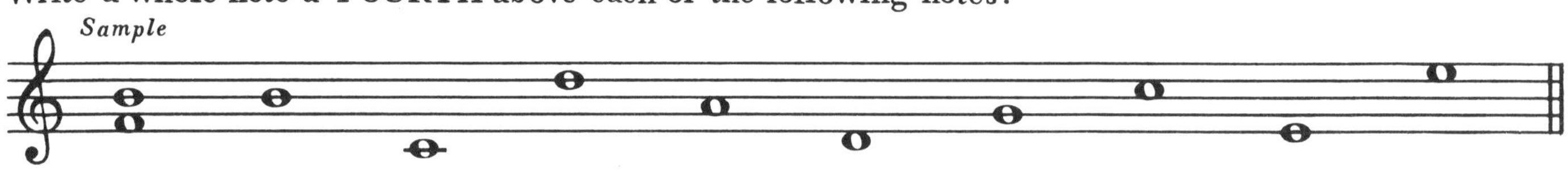

Write a whole note a FIFTH above each of the following notes.

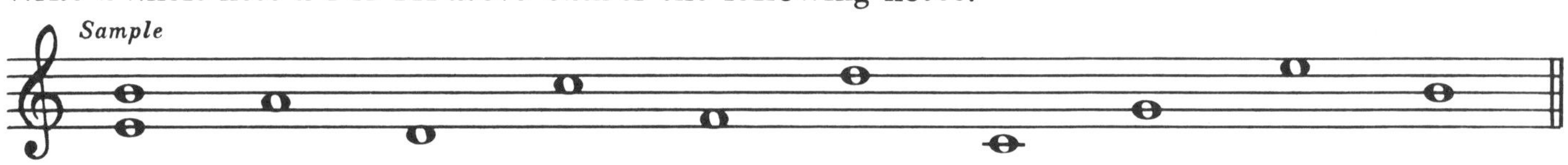

Write a whole note a SIXTH above each of the following notes.

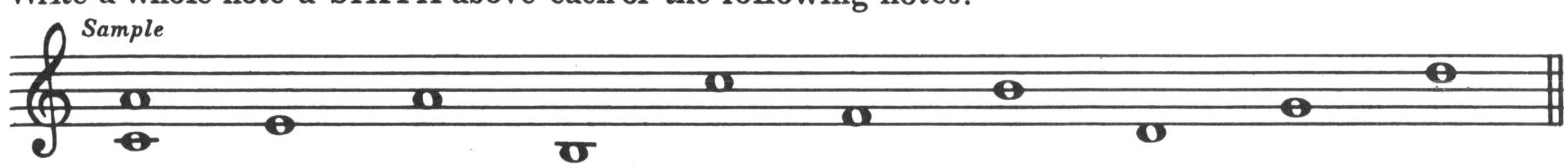

Write a whole note a SEVENTH above each of the following notes.

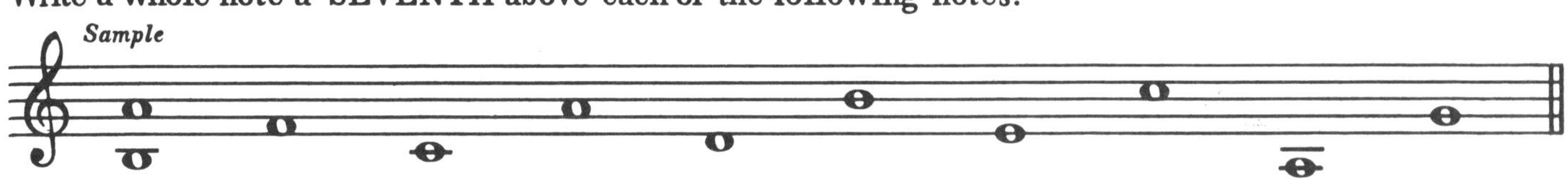

Write a whole note an OCTAVE above each of the following notes.

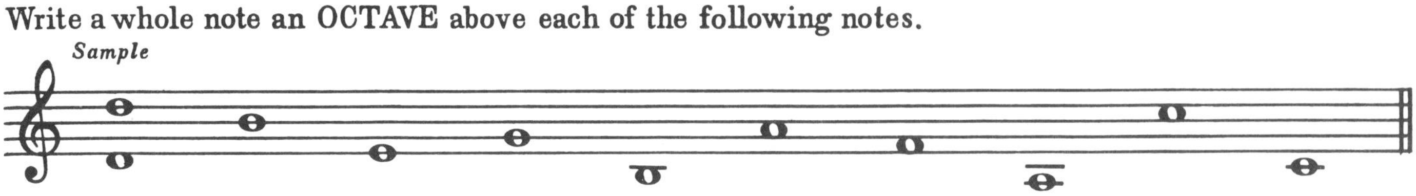

Teacher's Note: All intervals throughout the book should be performed at the keyboard so that the ear as well as the eye is trained.

Lesson 3. Interval Construction (Sharp Keys)

Pupil's Name.. Completion Date..

Assignment Date.. Grade or Star..

The major scale is the standard of measurement for intervals. On the staffs below, the TONIC (first note of scale) is always given. Intervals are formed by computing from the TONIC upward.

DIRECTIONS: Above each of the whole notes on the following staffs, write the correct note that makes the specified interval. Also write the letter names on the dotted lines. Study the samples.

C

Samples

Second Third Fourth Fifth Sixth Seventh Octave

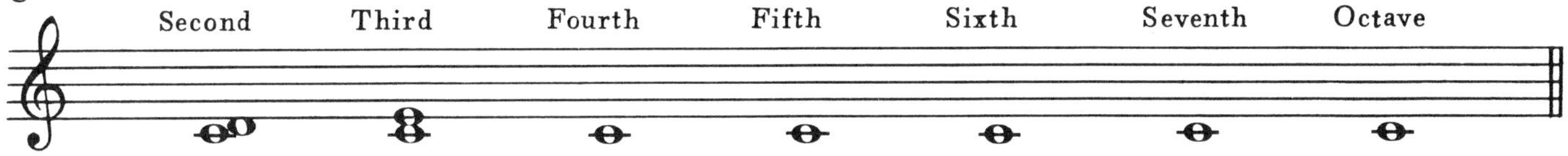

C D C E

(*Write letter names*)

G

Second Third Fourth Fifth Sixth Seventh Octave

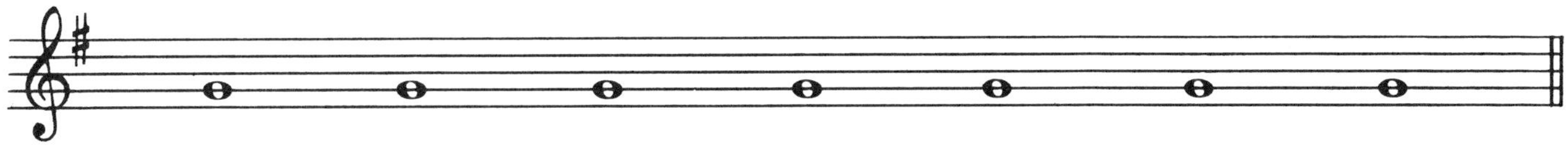

(*Write letter names*)

D

Second Third Fourth Fifth Sixth Seventh Octave

(*Write letter names*)

A

Second Third Fourth Fifth Sixth Seventh Octave

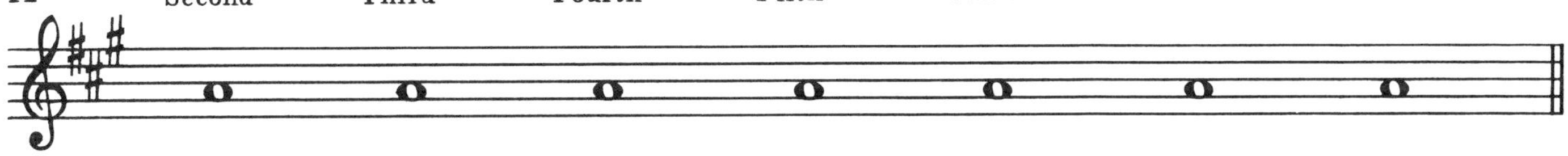

(*Write letter names*)

E

Second Third Fourth Fifth Sixth Seventh Octave

(*Write letter names*)

B

Second Third Fourth Fifth Sixth Seventh Octave

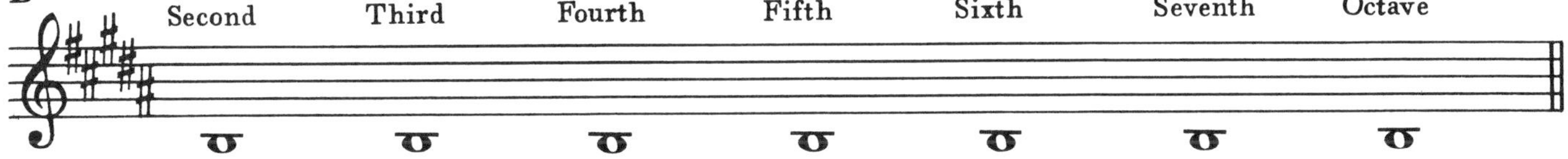

(*Write letter names*)

Teacher's Note: The UNISON or PRIME  *is, strictly speaking, not an interval at all since there is no difference in pitch. Consequently, it will not be presented in the book.*

Lesson 4. Interval Construction (Flat Keys)

Pupil's Name.. Completion Date..

Assignment Date.. Grade or Star..

DIRECTIONS: Above each of the whole notes on the following staffs, write the correct note that makes the specified interval. Also write the letter names on the dotted lines. Study the samples.

F

Samples: Second, Third | Fourth | Fifth | Sixth | Seventh | Octave

F G .... F A ....

(*Write letter names*)

B♭

Second | Third | Fourth | Fifth | Sixth | Seventh | Octave

....

(*Write letter names*)

E♭

Second | Third | Fourth | Fifth | Sixth | Seventh | Octave

....

(*Write letter names*)

A♭

Second | Third | Fourth | Fifth | Sixth | Seventh | Octave

....

(*Write letter names*)

D♭

Second | Third | Fourth | Fifth | Sixth | Seventh | Octave

....

(*Write letter names*)

G♭

Second | Third | Fourth | Fifth | Sixth | Seventh | Octave

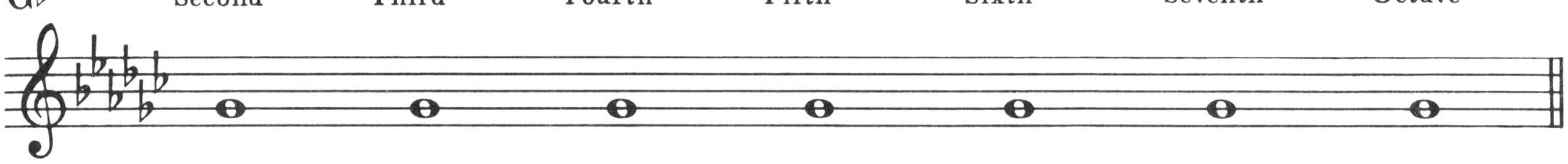

....

(*Write letter names*)

Lesson 5. Normal Intervals *(Sharp Keys)*

Pupil's Name.. *Completion Date*..

Assignment Date.. *Grade or Star*..

The term NORMAL applies to an interval which can be formed from the TONIC to any other degree of the major scale. The SECONDS, THIRDS, SIXTHS and SEVENTHS so constructed are labeled MAJOR. The FOURTHS, FIFTHS and OCTAVES are named PERFECT. The precise difference between MAJOR and PERFECT will be explained later.

DIRECTIONS: Above each of the TONIC whole notes on the following staffs, write the correct note that produces the designated interval. Write the number of half steps contained in each interval on the dotted lines. The amount of half steps in an interval determines its kind or variety. The key of C is already marked as it should be.

C

Major Second | Major Third | Perfect Fourth | Perfect Fifth | Major Sixth | Major Seventh | Perfect Octave

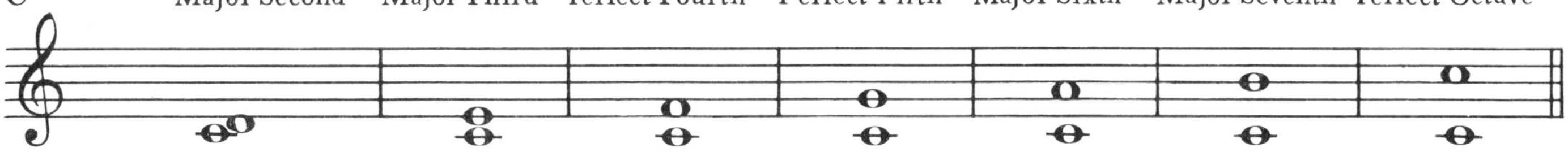

2 | 4 | 5 | 7 | 9 | 11 | 12

(Number of half steps)

G

Major Second | Major Third | Perfect Fourth | Perfect Fifth | Major Sixth | Major Seventh | Perfect Octave

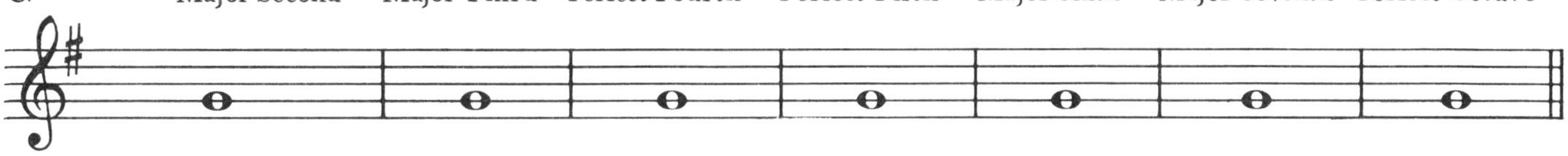

....

(Number of half steps)

D

Major Second | Major Third | Perfect Fourth | Perfect Fifth | Major Sixth | Major Seventh | Perfect Octave

....

(Number of half steps)

A

Major Second | Major Third | Perfect Fourth | Perfect Fifth | Major Sixth | Major Seventh | Perfect Octave

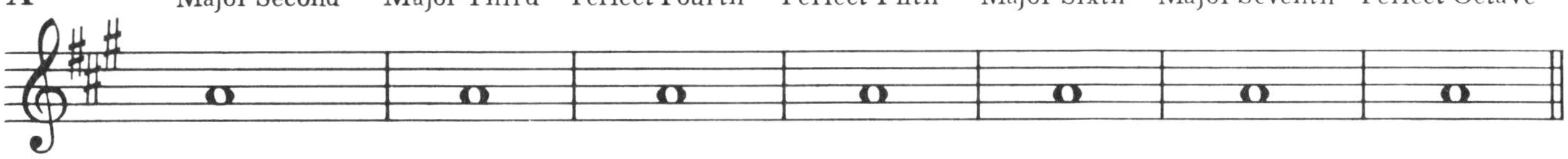

....

(Number of half steps)

E

Major Second | Major Third | Perfect Fourth | Perfect Fifth | Major Sixth | Major Seventh | Perfect Octave

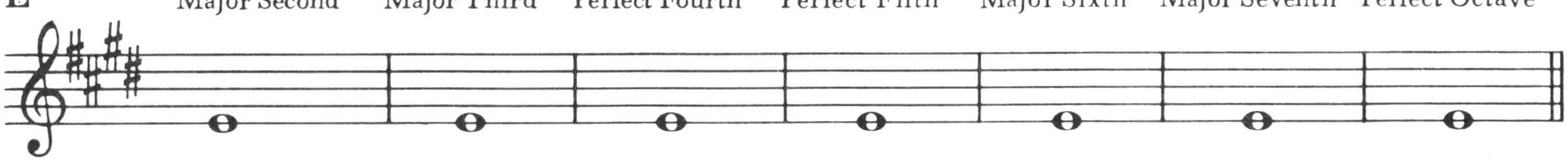

....

(Number of half steps)

B

Major Second | Major Third | Perfect Fourth | Perfect Fifth | Major Sixth | Major Seventh | Perfect Octave

....

(Number of half steps)

Lesson 6. Normal Intervals *(Flat Keys)*

Pupil's Name.. *Completion Date*..

Assignment Date.. *Grade or Star*..

DIRECTIONS: Above each of the TONIC whole notes on the following staffs, write the proper note that makes the specified interval. Write the number of half steps contained in each interval on the dotted lines.

F

Major Second | Major Third | Perfect Fourth | Perfect Fifth | Major Sixth | Major Seventh | Perfect Octave

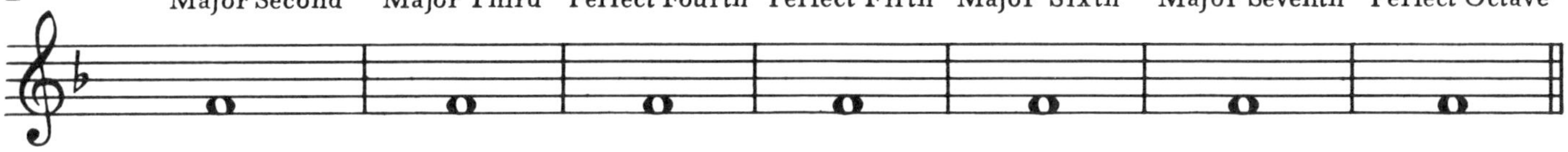

....

(Number of half steps)

B♭

Major Second | Major Third | Perfect Fourth | Perfect Fifth | Major Sixth | Major Seventh | Perfect Octave

....

(Number of half steps)

E♭

Major Second | Major Third | Perfect Fourth | Perfect Fifth | Major Sixth | Major Seventh | Perfect Octave

....

(Number of half steps)

A♭

Major Second | Major Third | Perfect Fourth | Perfect Fifth | Major Sixth | Major Seventh | Perfect Octave

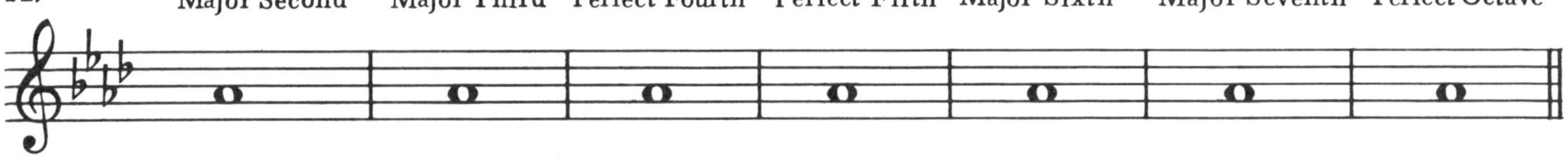

....

(Number of half steps)

D♭

Major Second | Major Third | Perfect Fourth | Perfect Fifth | Major Sixth | Major Seventh | Perfect Octave

....

(Number of half steps)

G♭

Major Second | Major Third | Perfect Fourth | Perfect Fifth | Major Sixth | Major Seventh | Perfect Octave

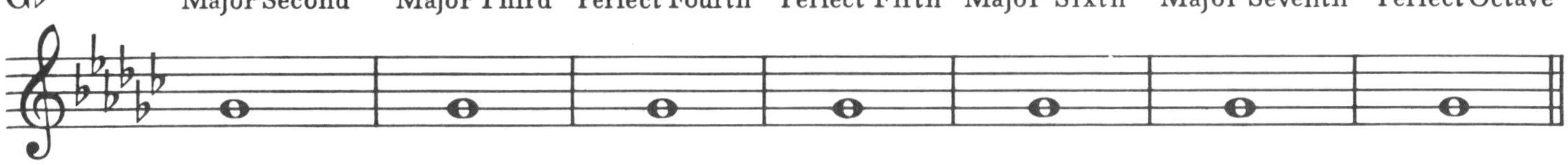

....

(Number of half steps)

Lesson 7. Interval Identification

Pupil's Name.. Completion Date..

Assignment Date.. Grade or Star..

DIRECTIONS: Below is a series of NORMAL intervals. Write the kind and number name of each of these intervals. Use the letter P for perfect and M for major. Thus, P4 means Perfect Fourth and M6 designates Major Sixth, etc. Remember that all seconds, thirds, sixths and sevenths formed from the tonic of any major scale are invariably MAJOR INTERVALS. In like manner, all fourths, fifths and octaves constructed from the tonic of any major scale are always PERFECT INTERVALS.

P4 M6 M3 P8

(Write kind and number name of each interval)

(Write kind and number name of each interval)

(Write kind and number name of each interval)

(Write kind and number name of each interval)

(Write kind and number name of each interval)

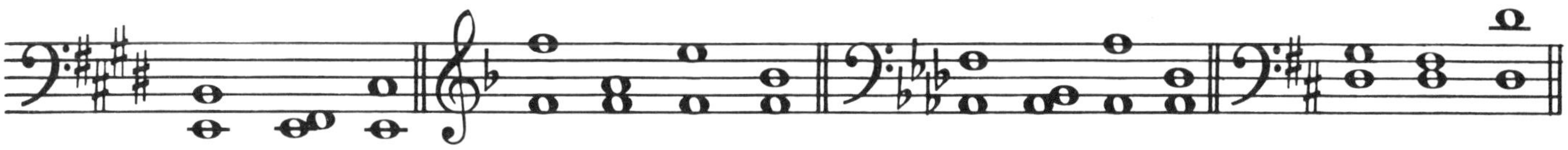

(Write kind and number name of each interval)

Lesson 8. Perfect Interval Analysis

Pupil's Name.. Completion Date..

Assignment Date.. Grade or Star..

Perfect intervals are those in which the upper note is found in the major scale of the lower note, and also the lower note is located in the major scale of the upper note. Notice the interval in Ex. 1. It is a PERFECT 5th because the upper note B♭ is found in the major scale of the lower note E♭ (Ex. 2) and also because the lower note E♭ is found in the major scale of the upper note B♭ (Ex. 3).

Ex. 1 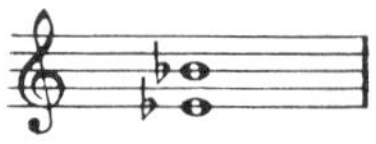
Perfect 5th

Ex. 2 
E♭ B♭

Ex. 3 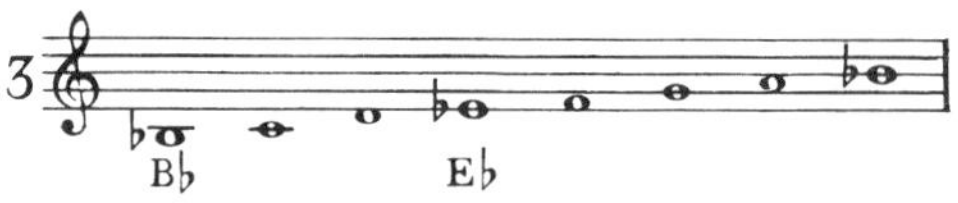
B♭ E♭

It is obvious that an octave will be perfect because both upper and lower notes have the same letter name and are automatically in the same scale.

DIRECTIONS: Analyze each of the following intervals by writing the answers on the dotted lines. Then test them on the keyboard by playing the intervals and scales.

1. This 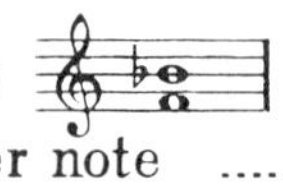 is a PERFECT ....; because the top note .... is in the major scale of the lower note ....; and the bottom note .... is in the major scale of the upper note ....

2. This  is a PERFECT ....; because the top note .... is in the major scale of the lower note ....; and the bottom note .... is in the major scale of the upper note ....

3. This  is a PERFECT ....; because the top note .... is in the major scale of the lower note ....; and the bottom note .... is in the major scale of the upper note ....

4. This 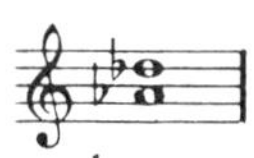 is a PERFECT ....; because the top note .... is in the major scale of the lower note ....; and the bottom note .... is in the major scale of the upper note ....

5. This  is a PERFECT ....; because the top note .... is in the major scale of the lower note ....; and the bottom note .... is in the major scale of the upper note ....

6. This  is a PERFECT ....; because the top note .... is in the major scale of the lower note ....; and the bottom note .... is in the major scale of the upper note ....

7. This 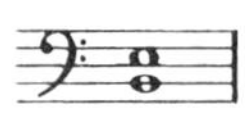 is a PERFECT ....; because the top note .... is in the major scale of the lower note ....; and the bottom note .... is in the major scale of the upper note ....

8. This 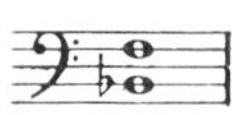 is a PERFECT ....; because the top note .... is in the major scale of the lower note ....; and the bottom note .... is in the major scale of the upper note ....

9. This  is a PERFECT ....; because the top note .... is in the major scale of the lower note ....; and the bottom note .... is in the major scale of the upper note ....

10. This 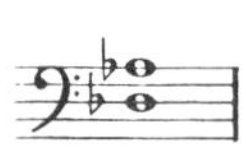 is a PERFECT ....; because the top note .... is in the major scale of the lower note ....; and the bottom note .... is in the major scale of the upper note ....

Lesson 9. Major Interval Analysis

Pupil's Name... *Completion Date*...

Assignment Date... *Grade or Star*...

An interval is MAJOR when the upper note is found in the major scale of the lower note, and the bottom note is NOT found in the major scale of the top note. Notice the interval in Ex.1. It is a MAJOR 6th because the upper note F is found in the major scale of the lower note A♭ (Ex.2.) and the bottom note A♭ is NOT found in the major scale of the top note F (Ex.3.)

Ex.1 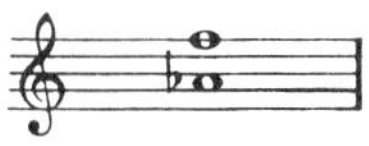
Major 6th

Ex.2 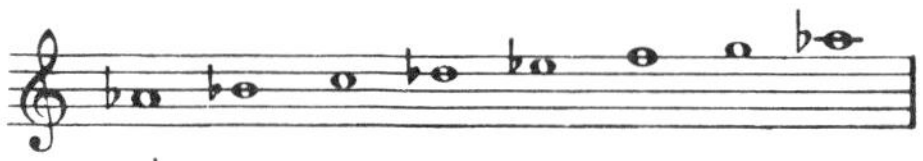
A♭ F

Ex.3 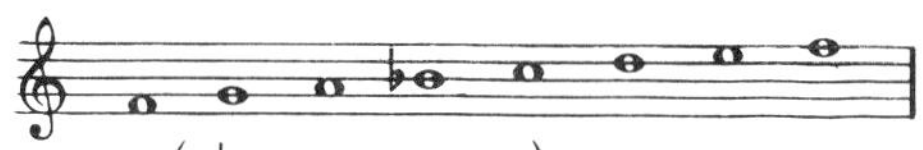
F (A♭ not in F major)

DIRECTIONS: Analyze each of the following intervals by writing the answers on the dotted lines. Then test them on the keyboard by playing the intervals and scales.

1. This  is a MAJOR ....; because the upper note .... is in the major scale of the bottom note ....; and the lower note .... is NOT in the major scale of the top note.........

2. This 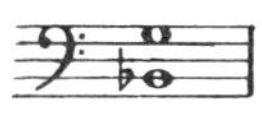 is a MAJOR ....; because the upper note .... is in the major scale of the bottom note ....; and the lower note .... is NOT in the major scale of the top note.........

3. This  is a MAJOR ....; because the upper note .... is in the major scale of the bottom note ....; and the lower note .... is NOT in the major scale of the top note.........

4. This  is a MAJOR ....; because the upper note .... is in the major scale of the bottom note ....; and the lower note .... is NOT in the major scale of the top note.........

5. This 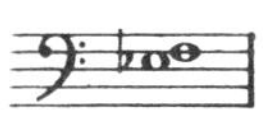 is a MAJOR ....; because the upper note .... is in the major scale of the bottom note ....; and the lower note .... is NOT in the major scale of the top note.........

6. This  is a MAJOR ....; because the upper note .... is in the major scale of the bottom note ....; and the lower note .... is NOT in the major scale of the top note.........

7. This 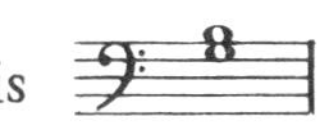 is a MAJOR ....; because the upper note .... is in the major scale of the bottom note ....; and the lower note .... is NOT in the major scale of the top note.........

8. This  is a MAJOR ....; because the upper note .... is in the major scale of the bottom note ....; and the lower note .... is NOT in the major scale of the top note.........

9. This  is a MAJOR ....; because the upper note .... is in the major scale of the bottom note ....; and the lower note .... is NOT in the major scale of the top note.........

10. This  is a MAJOR ....; because the upper note .... is in the major scale of the bottom note ....; and the lower note .... is NOT in the major scale of the top note.........

Lesson 10. Minor Intervals (Sharp Keys)

Pupil's Name .... Completion Date ....

Assignment Date .... Grade or Star ....

When the top note of a major interval is lowered a half step, it becomes a MINOR interval. The letter names, of course, must remain unchanged. Major intervals exclusively can become minor. Perfect intervals have no minor form. Therefore, you will find that only seconds, thirds, sixths and sevenths are minor.

DIRECTIONS: On the following staffs, insert wherever necessary the proper accidental (♯, ♭ or ♮) sign before the UPPER note of each interval to produce the exact type of interval specified above each measure. On the dotted lines, write the number of half steps contained in each interval. The intervals on the first staff are already marked as they should be. Frequently, both major and minor intervals will require an accidental sign. For example, notice the last two measures on the second staff. To make the major 7th, the F must be sharped and to produce the minor 7th, the F will become natural.

C

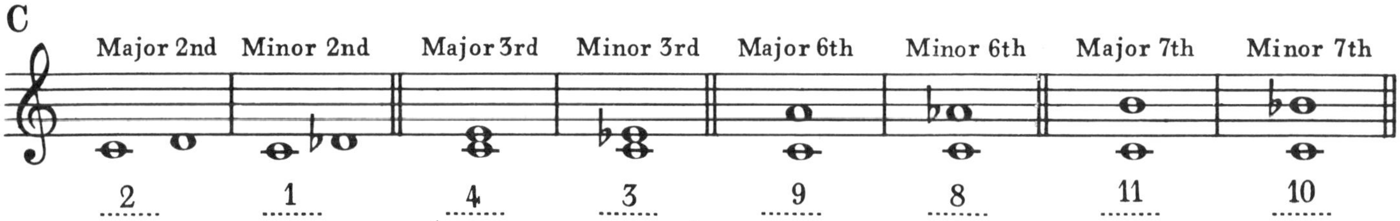

(Write number of half steps)

G

(Write number of half steps)

D

(Write number of half steps)

A

(Write number of half steps)

E

(Write number of half steps)

B

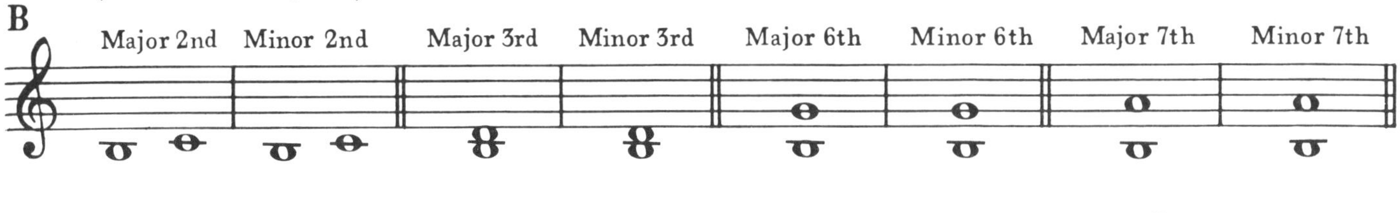

(Write number of half steps)

Lesson 11. Minor Intervals (Flat Keys)

Pupil's Name.. Completion Date..

Assignment Date.. Grade or Star..

DIRECTIONS: On the following staffs, insert wherever necessary the proper accidental (♯,♭,𝄫 or ♮) sign in front of the UPPER note of each interval to produce the exact type of interval specified above every measure. Quite often, both major and minor intervals will need an accidental sign. For example, look at the first two measures on the fourth staff. To make the major 2nd, the B must be flatted; and to form the minor 2nd the B must be double flatted. (𝄫)

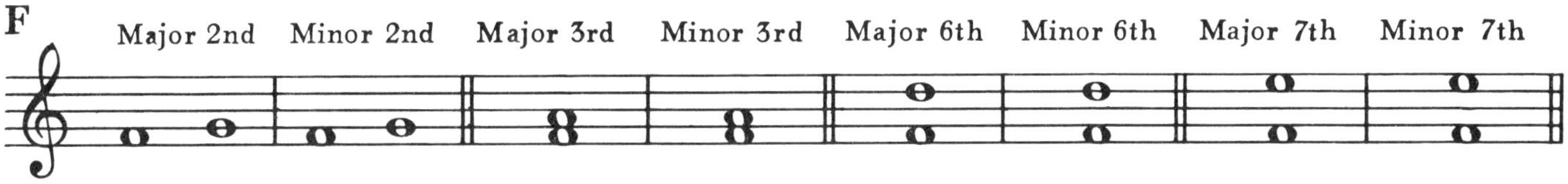

....

(Write number of half steps)

....

(Write number of half steps)

....

(Write number of half steps)

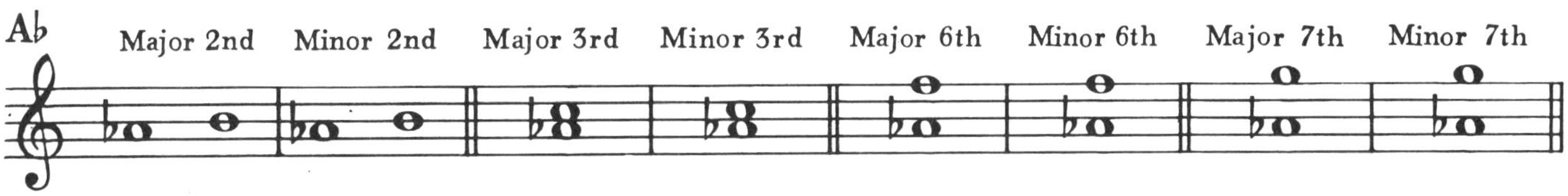

....

(Write number of half steps)

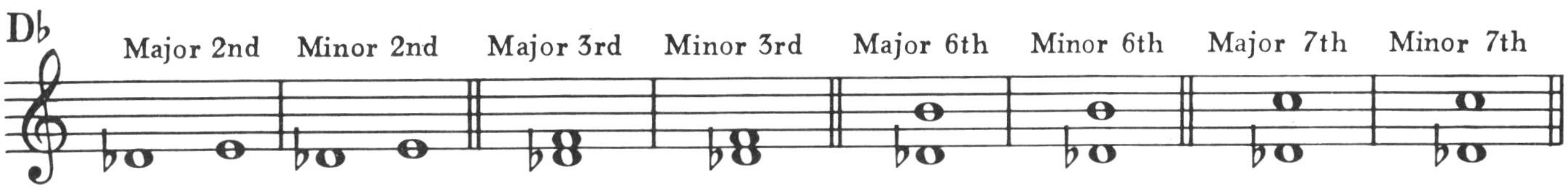

....

(Write number of half steps)

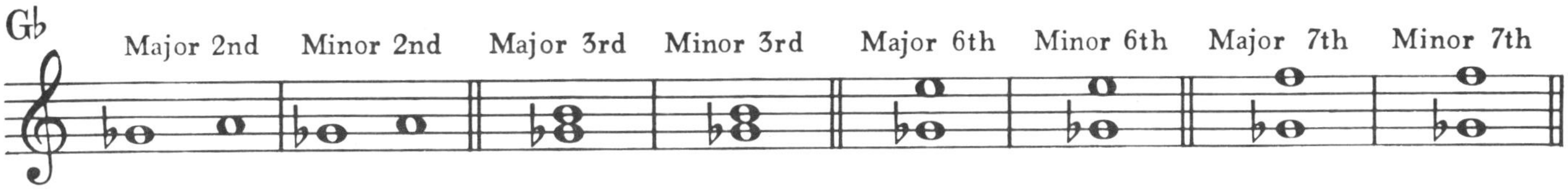

....

(Write number of half steps)

Lesson 12. Augmented Intervals

Pupil's Name.................................... Completion Date....................................

Assignment Date.................................... Grade or Star....................................

When the top note of a major or a perfect interval is raised a chromatic half step, the interval becomes AUGMENTED. Seconds, fourths, fifths and sixths are the only augmented intervals in practical use. Any interval which becomes perfect (in sound and number of half steps) through chromatic change should be altered to read perfect. An augmented 3rd would be the same (in sound and number of half steps) as a perfect 4th; likewise an augmented 7th would be the same as a perfect octave. Therefore, we discover that although these intervals are possible in theory, they rarely occur in actual music.

DIRECTIONS: An augmented interval is designated by a plus (+) sign. Thus, 2 + = an augmented second; 4 + = augmented fourth, etc. On the following staffs, insert wherever necessary the correct accidental sign in front of the UPPER note of each interval so that the specified augmented interval is formed. In some cases, a double sharp sign (×) will be needed.

....

(Write number of half steps)

....

(Write number of half steps)

....

(Write number of half steps)

....

(Write number of half steps)

....

(Write number of half steps)

....

(Write number of half steps)

Lesson 13. Diminished Intervals

Pupil's Name.. Completion Date..

Assignment Date.. Grade or Star..

When the top note of a perfect or minor interval is lowered a chromatic half step, the interval becomes DIMINISHED. Thirds, fourths, fifths and sevenths are the only diminished intervals in practical use. Any interval which becomes perfect (in sound) through chromatic change should be altered to read perfect. A diminished 2nd would be the same (in sound) as a perfect prime or unison; likewise a diminished 6th would be the same as a perfect 5th. Therefore, we discover that although these intervals are possible in theory, they rarely occur in actual music.

DIRECTIONS: A diminished interval is abbreviated as follows: 3° = a diminished third; 5° = a diminished fifth; etc. On the following staffs, insert wherever necessary the correct accidental sign in front of the UPPER note of each interval so that the specified diminished interval is formed. Remember: To make a major interval diminished, it must first be made minor and then the top note must be lowered another half step.

Sample: 3° 4° 5° 7° — 3° 4° 5° 7°

2 .... 4 .... 6 .... 9 .... — ....

(Write number of half steps)

3° 4° 5° 7° — 3° 4° 5° 7°

.... — ....

(Write number of half steps)

3° 4° 5° 7° — 3° 4° 5° 7°

.... — ....

(Write number of half steps)

3° 4° 5° 7° — 3° 4° 5° 7°

.... — ....

(Write number of half steps)

3° 4° 5° 7° — 3° 4° 5° 7°

.... — ....

(Write number of half steps)

3° 4° 5° 7° — 3° 4° 5° 7°

.... — ....

(Write number of half steps)

Note: In the key of G♭, the upper note of the diminished third will be B triple flat: 

Lesson 14. Table of Intervals (Sharp Keys—Part 1)

Pupil's Name.. Completion Date..

Assignment Date.. Grade or Star..

Below is a complete Table of Intervals in the scale of C major. The intervals given are those that occur in practical use, the purely theoretical ones have been omitted. All the accidental signs are properly inserted and the number of half steps are correctly placed on the dotted lines. Use this as a model in preparing the Table of Intervals for all the other major scales.

C

Seconds: Major, Minor, Augmented — Thirds: Major, Minor, Diminished — Fourths: Perfect, Augmented, Diminished

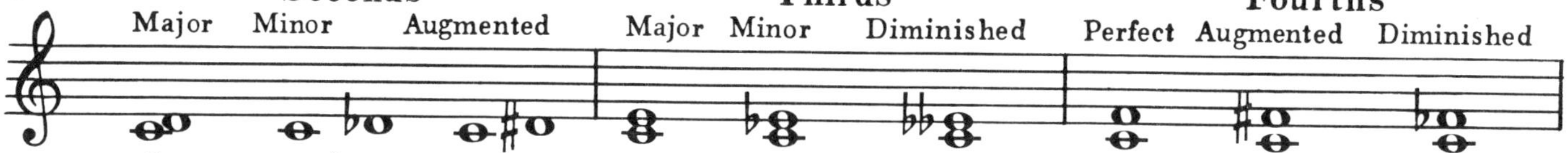

2 1 3 4 3 2 5 6 4

(Number of half steps)

Fifths: Perfect, Augmented, Diminished — Sixths: Major, Minor, Augmented — Sevenths: Major, Minor, Diminished

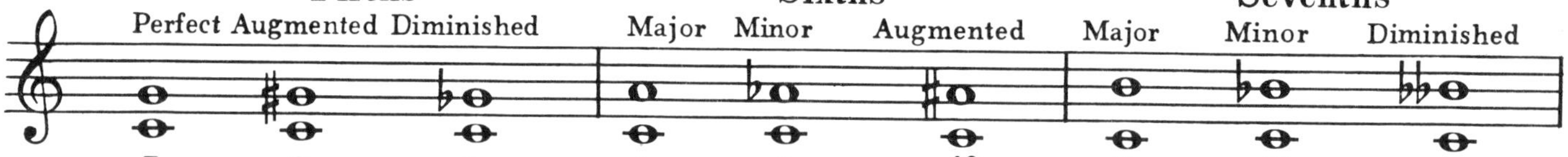

7 8 6 9 8 10 11 10 9

(Number of half steps)

DIRECTIONS: On the following staffs, insert wherever necessary the correct accidental sign in front of the UPPER note of each interval to produce the exact type of interval specified above each example. Use the key of C major as a guide.

G

Seconds: Major, Minor, Augmented — Thirds: Major, Minor, Diminished — Fourths: Perfect, Augmented, Diminished

....

(Write number of half steps)

Fifths: Perfect, Augmented, Diminished — Sixths: Major, Minor, Augmented — Sevenths: Major, Minor, Diminished

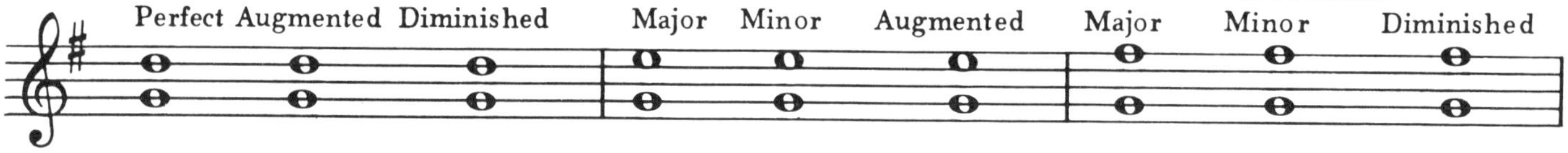

....

(Write number of half steps)

D

Seconds: Major, Minor, Augmented — Thirds: Major, Minor, Diminished — Fourths: Perfect, Augmented, Diminished

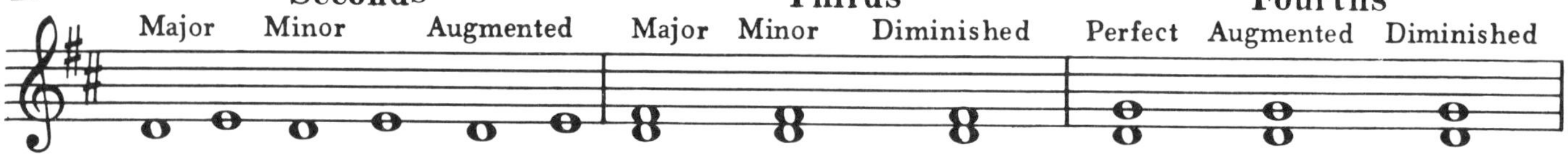

....

(Write number of half steps)

Fifths: Perfect, Augmented, Diminished — Sixths: Major, Minor, Augmented — Sevenths: Major, Minor, Diminished

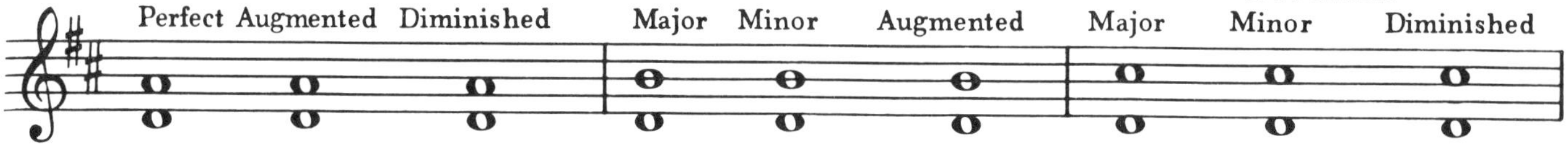

....

(Write number of half steps)

Lesson 15. Table of Intervals (Sharp Keys—Part 2)

Pupil's Name.. Completion Date..

Assignment Date.. Grade or Star..

DIRECTIONS: On the following staffs, insert wherever necessary the correct accidental sign in front of the UPPER note of each interval to produce the exact type of interval specified above each example. Use the key of C major on page 16 as a model.

A

Seconds — Major, Minor, Augmented | **Thirds** — Major, Minor, Diminished | **Fourths** — Perfect, Augmented, Diminished

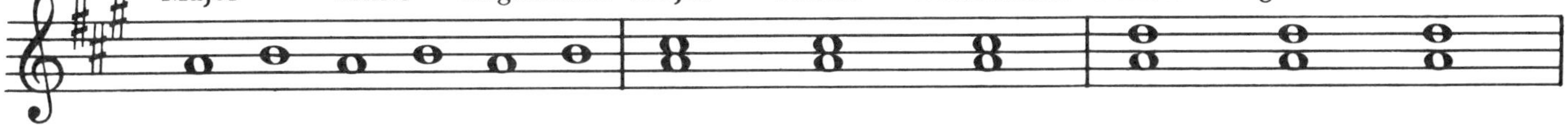

(Write number of half steps)

Fifths — Perfect, Augmented, Diminished | **Sixths** — Major, Minor, Augmented | **Sevenths** — Major, Minor, Diminished

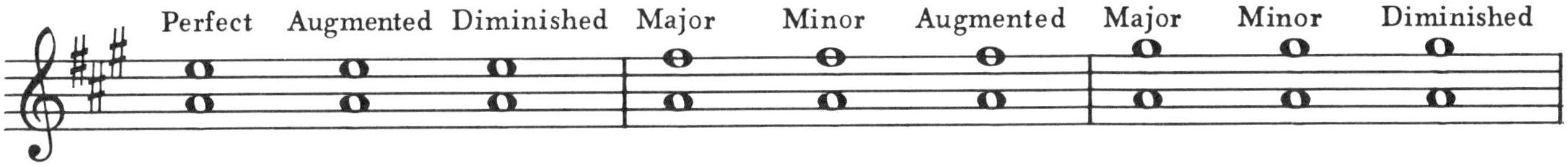

(Write number of half steps)

E

Seconds — Major, Minor, Augmented | **Thirds** — Major, Minor, Diminished | **Fourths** — Perfect, Augmented, Diminished

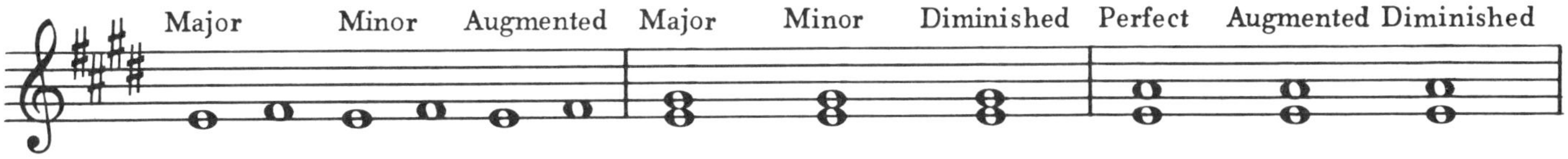

(Write number of half steps)

Fifths — Perfect, Augmented, Diminished | **Sixths** — Major, Minor, Augmented | **Sevenths** — Major, Minor, Diminished

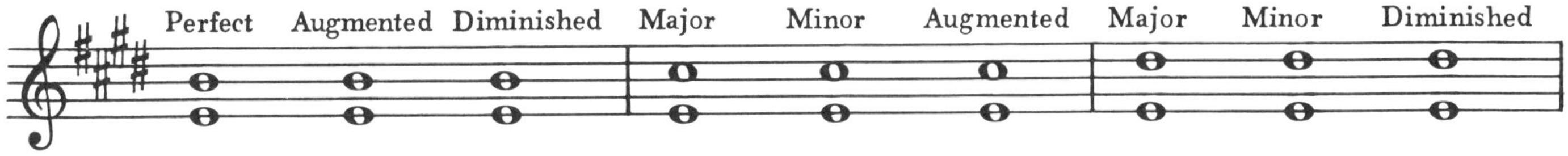

(Write number of half steps)

B

Seconds — Major, Minor, Augmented | **Thirds** — Major, Minor, Diminished | **Fourths** — Perfect, Augmented, Diminished

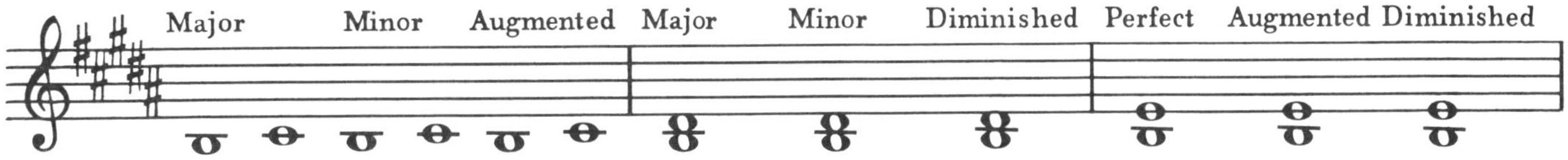

(Write number of half steps)

Fifths — Perfect, Augmented, Diminished | **Sixths** — Major, Minor, Augmented | **Sevenths** — Major, Minor, Diminished

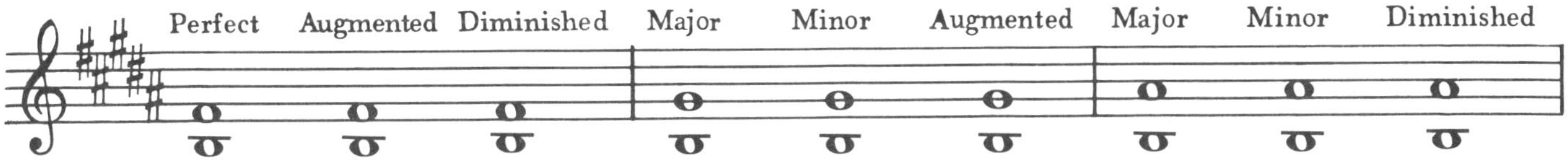

(Write number of half steps)

Lesson 16. Table of Intervals (Flat Keys—Part 1)

Pupil's Name.. Completion Date..

Assignment Date.. Grade or Star..

DIRECTIONS: On the following staffs, insert wherever necessary the **proper** accidental sign in front of the UPPER note of each interval to produce the exact type of interval specified above each example. Use the key of C major on page 16 as a model.

F

Seconds			Thirds			Fourths		
Major	Minor	Augmented	Major	Minor	Diminished	Perfect	Augmented	Diminished

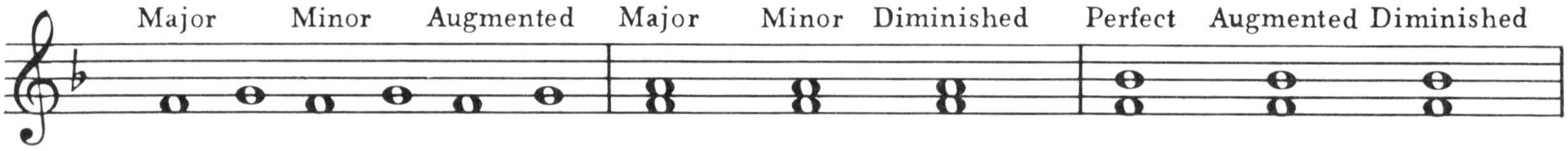

(Write number of half steps)

Fifths			Sixths			Sevenths		
Perfect	Augmented	Diminished	Major	Minor	Augmented	Major	Minor	Diminished

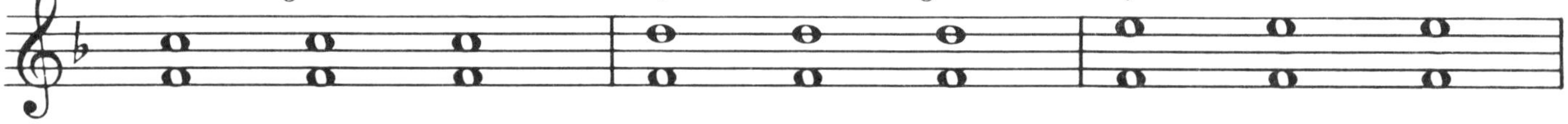

(Write number of half steps)

B♭

Seconds			Thirds			Fourths		
Major	Minor	Augmented	Major	Minor	Diminished	Perfect	Augmented	Diminished

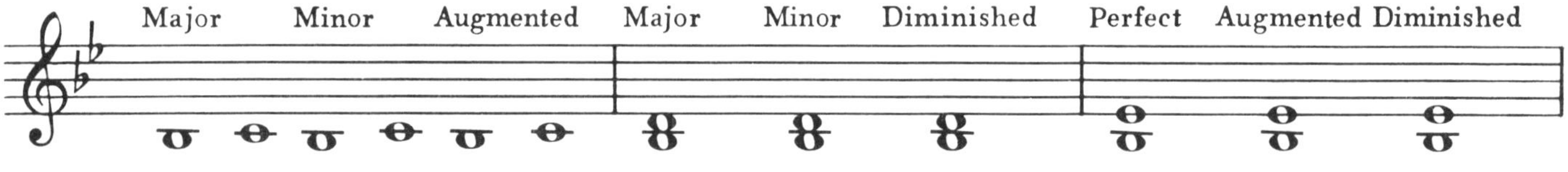

(Write number of half steps)

Fifths			Sixths			Sevenths		
Perfect	Augmented	Diminished	Major	Minor	Augmented	Major	Minor	Diminished

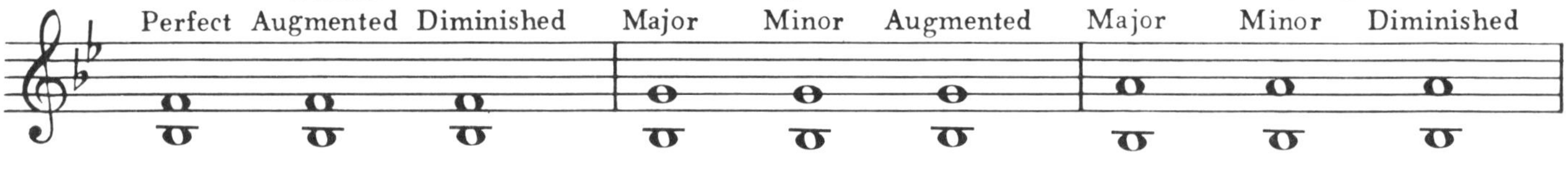

(Write number of half steps)

E♭

Seconds			Thirds			Fourths		
Major	Minor	Augmented	Major	Minor	Diminished	Perfect	Augmented	Diminished

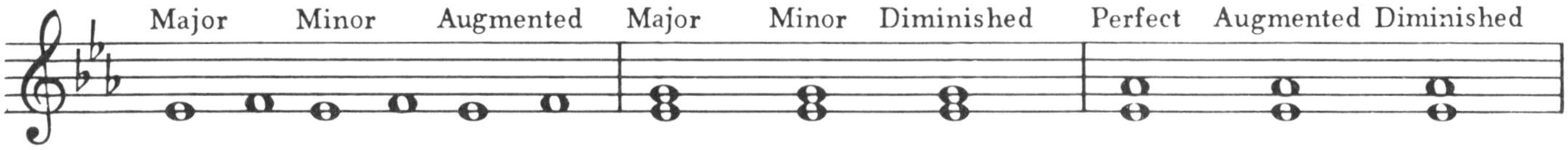

(Write number of half steps)

Fifths			Sixths			Sevenths		
Perfect	Augmented	Diminished	Major	Minor	Augmented	Major	Minor	Diminished

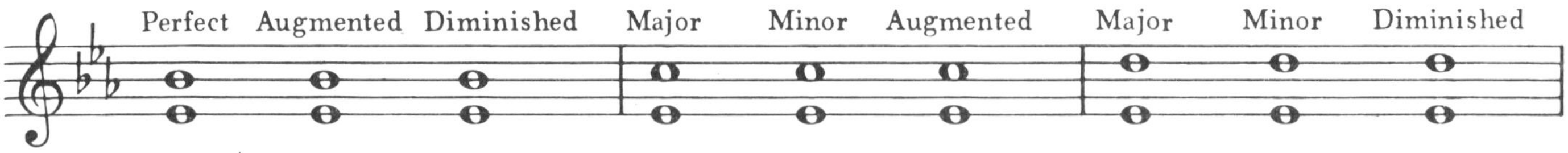

(Write number of half steps)

Lesson 17. Table of Intervals (Flat Keys—Part 2)

Pupil's Name.. Completion Date..

Assignment Date.. Grade or Star..

DIRECTIONS: On the following staffs, insert wherever necessary the proper accidental sign in front of the UPPER note of each interval to produce the exact type of interval specified above each example. Use the key of C major on page 16 as a model.

A♭

Seconds — Major, Minor, Augmented; **Thirds** — Major, Minor, Diminished; **Fourths** — Perfect, Augmented, Diminished

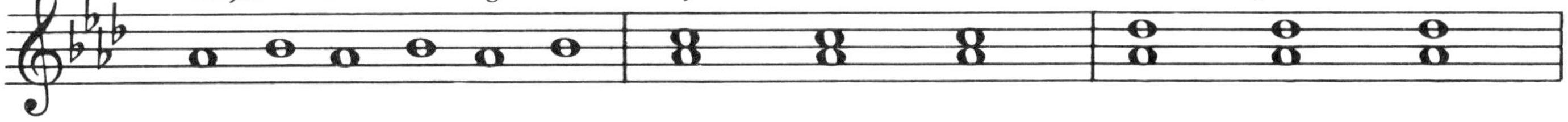

(*Write number of half steps*)

Fifths — Perfect, Augmented, Diminished; **Sixths** — Major, Minor, Augmented; **Sevenths** — Major, Minor, Diminished

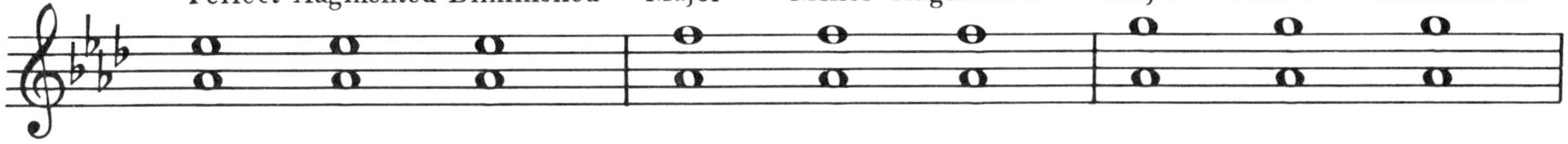

(*Write number of half steps*)

D♭

Seconds — Major, Minor, Augmented; **Thirds** — Major, Minor, Diminished; **Fourths** — Perfect, Augmented, Diminished

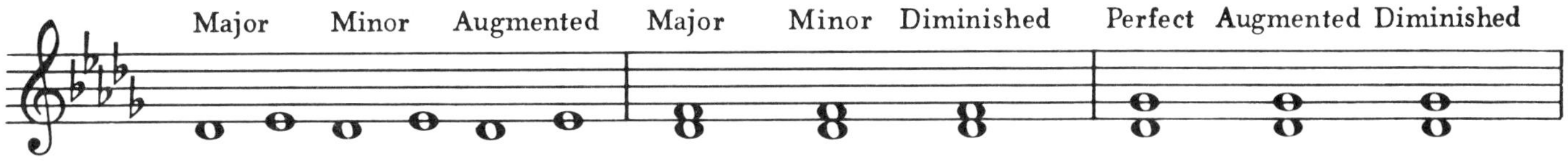

(*Write number of half steps*)

Fifths — Perfect, Augmented, Diminished; **Sixths** — Major, Minor, Augmented; **Sevenths** — Major, Minor, Diminished

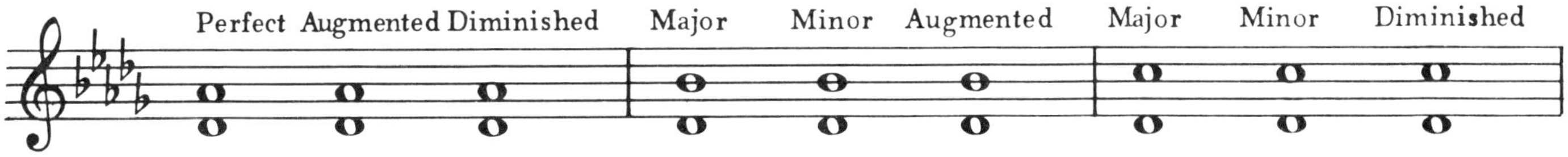

(*Write number of half steps*)

G♭

Seconds — Major, Minor, Augmented; **Thirds** — Major, Minor, Diminished; **Fourths** — Perfect, Augmented, Diminished

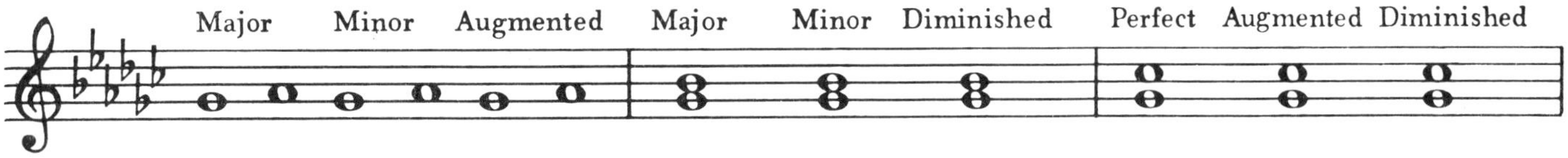

(*Write number of half steps*)

Fifths — Perfect, Augmented, Diminished; **Sixths** — Major, Minor, Augmented; **Sevenths** — Major, Minor, Diminished

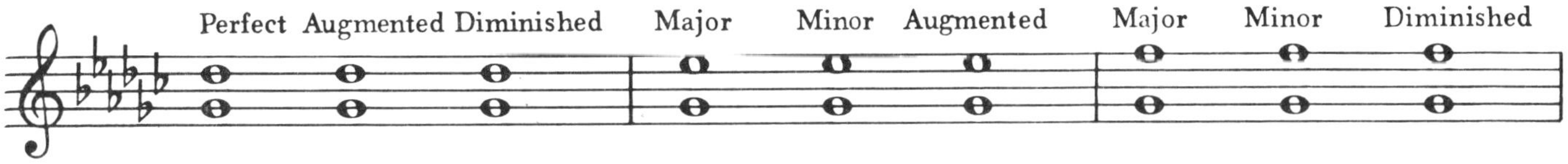

(*Write number of half steps*)

Lesson 18. Interval Recognition

Pupil's Name.. Completion Date..

Assignment Date.. Grade or Star..

DIRECTIONS: On the dotted lines below the following staffs, write the kind and number name of each interval. Use the abbreviations as shown in the samples. Major = M; minor = m; perfect = P; augmented = +; and diminished = ○.

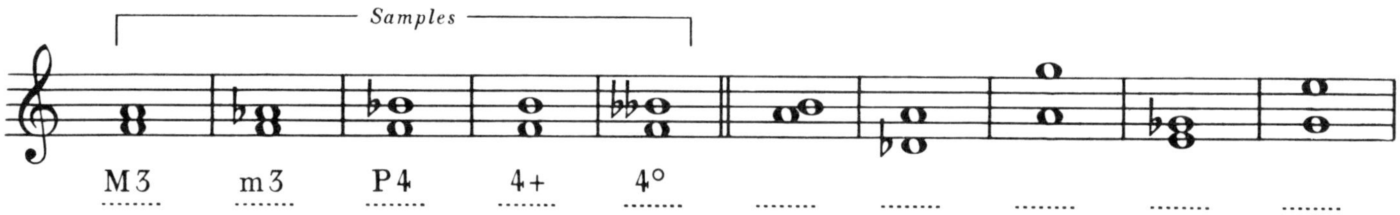

Lesson 19. Numerical Inversion of Intervals

Pupil's Name.. *Completion Date*..

Assignment Date.. *Grade or Star*..

To invert an interval, the notes must change their relative positions. The top note becomes the root (bottom note) and the root becomes the top note. For example:

This interval 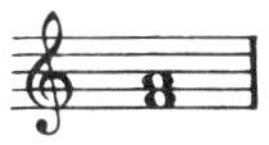 when inverted becomes 

DIRECTIONS: In the following measures, write out the inversion after each interval. Place the number name on the dotted line. As you do the exercises, observe that when you add together the lower note of the interval and the higher note of its inversion, you derive an octave.

REVIEW: At the keyboard, invert the intervals in Lessons 5 and 6. You will observe that whenever any major interval is inverted it produces a minor interval. Also notice that a perfect interval when invert-ed always produces another perfect interval.

Lesson 20. Computation of Intervals

Pupil's Name.. *Completion Date*..

Assignment Date.. *Grade or Star*..

To compute the name and kind of an interval, the lower note (root) must always be treated as the TONIC of a major scale, regardless of the key signature. The numerical distance of the upper tone from the tonic determines the name of the interval. If the upper note is in the major scale of the lower note (tonic) the interval is either perfect or major. If not, it is augmented, minor or diminished according to the explanations in Lessons 10 through 13.

DIRECTIONS: Compute the name and kind of each of the following intervals.

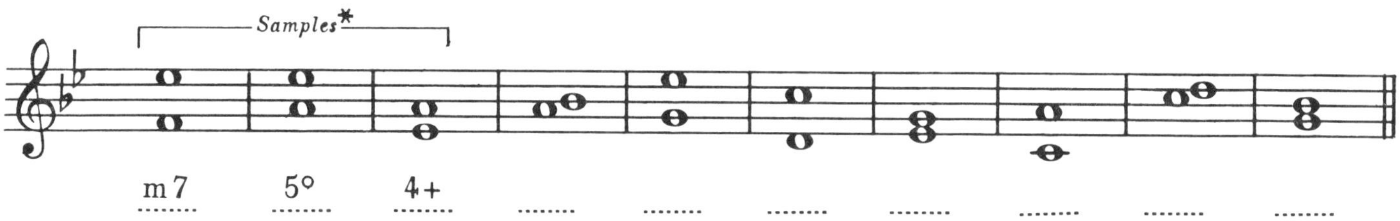

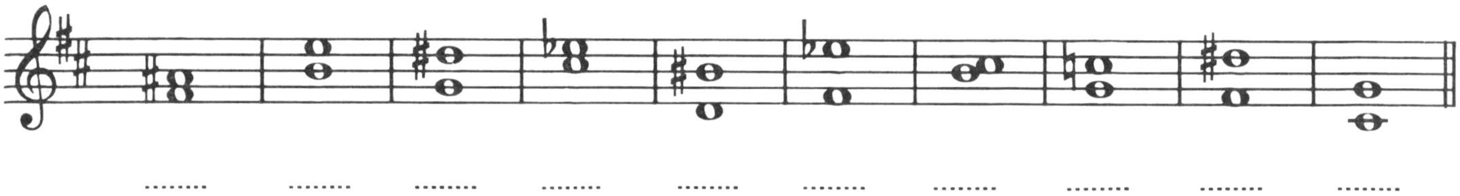

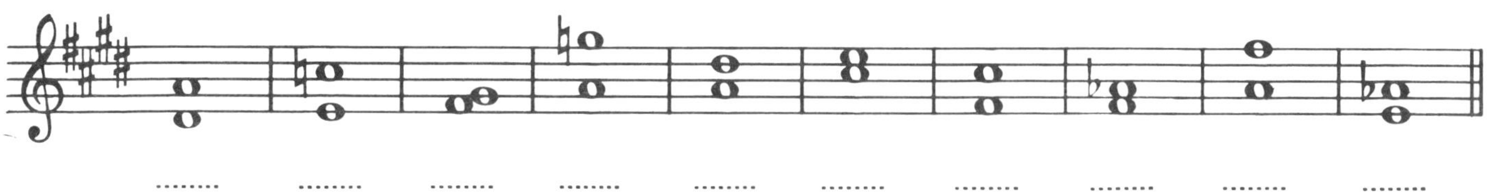

*** The key signatures apply to each measure throughout the entire staff. The accidental signs in the various measures are applicable only to the notes in a particular measure.**

You are now ready to progress to the Schaum **CHORD SPELLER**

Answer Page

Schaum Interval Speller

NOTE: TO CONSERVE THE TEACHER'S VALUABLE LESSON TIME, THE ANSWER PAGE IS INCLUDED. IT IS SUGGESTED THAT THE ANSWER PAGE BE REMOVED BEFORE THE STUDENT IS ASSIGNED THE BOOK.

Lesson 1

Line One: 3, 4, 5, 2, 7, 5, 7, 3.
Line Two: 8, 4, 6, 7, 3, 8, 6, 2, 5, 4.
Line Three: 7, 3, 5, 8, 4, 6, 2, 7, 3, 8.
Line Four: 2, 8, 4, 3, 7, 5, 4, 8, 2, 6.
Line Five: 4, 6, 2, 5, 8, 3, 6, 4, 7, 2.
Line Six: 5, 7, 8, 2, 3, 4, 6, 3, 8, 7.

Lesson 2

Note: The letter name of the upper note of each interval is given below.
Line One: A, G, C, E, F, B, D, G, F.
Line Two: G, G, C, B, A, F, D, A, F.
Line Three: E, F, G, D, G, C, F, A, A.
Line Four: E, A, G, C, A, G, D, B, F.
Line Five: C, F, G, A, D, G, B, E, B.
Line Six: E, B, G, C, A, D, B, G, F.
Line Seven: B, E, G, B, A, F, A, C, C.

Lesson 3

Key of C: CF, CG, CA, CB, CC.
Key of G: GA, GB, GC, GD, GE, GF♯, GG.
Key of D: DE, DF♯, DG, DA, DB, DC♯, DD.
Key of A: AB, AC♯, AD, AE, AF♯, AG♯, AA.
Key of E: EF♯, EG♯, EA, EB, EC♯, ED♯, EE.
Key of B: BC♯, BD♯, BE, BF♯, BG♯, BA♯, BB.

Lesson 4

Key of F: FB♭, FC, FD, FE, FF.
Key of B♭: B♭C, B♭D, B♭E♭, B♭F, B♭G, B♭A, B♭B♭.
Key of E♭: E♭F, E♭G, E♭A♭, E♭B♭, E♭C, E♭D, E♭E♭.
Key of A♭: A♭B♭, A♭C, A♭D♭, A♭E♭, A♭F, A♭G, A♭A♭.
Key of D♭: D♭E♭, D♭F, D♭G♭, D♭A♭, D♭B♭, D♭C, D♭D♭.
Key of G♭: G♭A♭, G♭B♭, G♭C♭, G♭D♭, G♭E♭, G♭F, G♭G♭.

Lesson 5

Explanatory Rules:
All major seconds always contain 2 half steps.
All major thirds always contain 4 half steps.
All perfect fourths always contain 5 half steps.
All perfect fifths always contain 7 half steps.
All major sixths always contain 9 half steps.
All major sevenths always contain 11 half steps.
All perfect octaves always contain 12 half steps.
Note: The letter name of the upper note of each interval is given below.
Key of G: A, B, C, D, E, F♯, G.
Key of D: E, F♯, G, A, B, C♯, D.
Key of A: B, C♯, D, E, F♯, G♯, A.
Key of E: F♯, G♯, A, B, C♯, D♯, E.
Key of B: C♯, D♯, E, F♯, G♯, A♯, B.

Lesson 6

Note: The explanatory rules for lesson 5 also apply here.
Key of F: G, A, B♭, C, D, E, F.
Key of B♭: C, D, E♭, F, G, A, B♭.
Key of E♭: F, G, A♭, B♭, C, D, E♭.
Key of A♭: B♭, C, D♭, E♭, F, G, A♭.
Key of D♭: E♭, F, G♭, A♭, B♭, C, D♭.
Key of G♭: A♭, B♭, C♭, D♭, E♭, F, G♭.

Lesson 7

Line 1 - P5, M3, M6; M2, P4, M6, M3; M7, M3, P5.
Line 2 - P5, M2, M6; M3, M7, P4, P8; M6, M2, M7, P5; M3, M7, P5.
Line 3 - M7, M3, P5; P4, P8, M6; M3, P5, M2, P8; P4, M7, M3, M6.
Line 4 - P4, P8, M2, M6; M7, P5, P8; P4, M6, M7; M7, P4, M2, P8.
Line 5 - M3, P5, M2, M7; P4, M2, P8, M6; M2, P5, P8; P5, M2, M7.
Line 6 - P5, M2, M6; P8, M3, M7, P4; M6, M2, P8, P4; P4, M3, P8.

Lesson 8

Line 1 - P4; B♭, F; F, B♭.
Line 2 - P5; E, A; A, E.
Line 3 - P4; G, D; D, G.
Line 4 - P4; D♭, A♭; A♭, D♭.
Line 5 - P5; B, E; E, B.
Line 6 - P5; D♭, G♭; G♭, D♭.
Line 7 - P4; E, B; B, E.
Line 8 - P5; F, B♭; B♭, F.
Line 9 - P4; A, E; E, A.
Line 10 - P5; A♭, D♭; D♭, A♭.

Lesson 9

Line 1 - M3; A, F; F, A.
Line 2 - M6; G, B♭; B♭, G.
Line 3 - M2; B, A; A, B.
Line 4 - M7; F, G♭; G♭, F.
Line 5 - M2; F, E♭; E♭, F.
Line 6 - M6; B♭, D♭; D♭, B♭.
Line 7 - M3; B, G; G, B.
Line 8 - M7; C♯, D; D, C♯.
Line 9 - M3; C, A♭; A♭, C.
Line 10 - M6; A, C; C, A.

Lesson 10

Explanatory Rules:
All major seconds always contain 2 half steps.
All minor seconds always contain 1 half step.
All major thirds always contain 4 half steps.
All minor thirds always contain 3 half steps.
All major sixths always contain 9 half steps.
All minor sixths always contain 8 half steps.
All major sevenths always contain 11 half steps.
All minor sevenths always contain 10 half steps.
Note: The letter name of the upper note of each interval is given below.
Key of G: A, A♭; B, B♭; E, E♭; F♯, F♮.
Key of D: E, E♭; F♯, F♮; B, B♭; C♯, C♮.
Key of A: B, B♭; C♯, C♮; F♯, F♮; G♯, G♮.
Key of E: F♯, F♮; G♯, G♮; C♯, C♮; D♯, D♮.
Key of B: C♯, C♮; D♯, D♮; G♯, G♮; A♯, A♮.

Lesson 11

Note: The explanatory rules for lesson 10 also apply here.

Key of F: G, Gb; A, Ab; D, Db; E, Eb.
Key of Bb: C, Cb; D, Db; G, Gb; A, Ab.
Key of Eb: F, Fb; G, Gb; C, Cb; D, Db.
Key of Ab: Bb, Bbb; C, Cb; F, Fb; G, Gb.
Key of Db: Eb, Ebb; F, Fb; Bb, Bbb; C, Cb.
Key of Gb: Ab, Abb; Bb, Bbb; Eb, Ebb; F, Fb.

Lesson 12

Explanatory Rules:
All augmented seconds always contain 3 half steps.
All augmented fourths always contain 6 half steps.
All augmented fifths always contain 8 half steps.
All augmented sixths always contain 10 half steps.
The top note of each interval is as follows.

Key of C: D#, F#, G#, A#.	Key of F: G#, B♮, C#, D#.
Key of G: A#, C#, D#, E#.	Key of B flat: C#, E♮, F#, G#.
Key of D: E#, G#, A#, B#.	Key of E flat: F#, A♮, B♮, C#.
Key of A: B#, D#, E#, F×.	Key of A flat: B♮, D♮, E♮, F#.
Key of E: F×, A#, B#, C×.	Key of D flat: E♮, G♮, A♮, B♮.
Key of B: C×, E#, F×, G×.	Key of G flat: A♮, C♮, D♮, E♮.

Lesson 13

Explanatory Rules:
All diminished thirds always contain 2 half steps.
All diminished fourths always contain 4 half steps.
All diminished fifths always contain 6 half steps.
All diminished sevenths always contain 9 half steps.
The top note of each interval is as follows:

Key of G: Bbb, Cb, Db, Fb.	Key of F: Abb, Bbb, Cb, Ebb.
Key of D: Fb, Gb, Ab, Cb.	Key of B flat: Dbb, Ebb, Fb, Abb.
Key of A: Cb, Db, Eb, Gb.	Key of E flat: Gbb, Abb, Bbb, Dbb.
Key of E: Gb, Ab, Bb, Db.	Key of A flat: Cbb, Dbb, Ebb, Gbb.
Key of B: Db, Eb, F♮, Ab.	Key of D flat: Fbb, Gbb, Abb, Cbb.
	Key of G flat: Bbbb, Cbb, Dbb, Fbb.

Lesson 14

Explanatory Rules:

SECONDS always contain:
Major = 2 half steps
minor = 1 half step
Augmented = 3 half steps

THIRDS always contain:
Major = 4 half steps
minor = 3 half steps
Diminished = 2 half steps

FOURTHS always contain:
Perfect = 5 half steps
Augmented = 6 half steps
Diminished = 4 half steps

FIFTHS always contain:
Perfect = 7 half steps
Augmented = 8 half steps
Diminished = 6 half steps

SIXTHS always contain:
Major = 9 half steps
minor = 8 half steps
Augmented = 10 half steps

SEVENTHS always contain:
Major = 11 half steps
minor = 10 half steps
Diminished = 9 half steps

Note: The top note of each interval is as follows:

Key of G:
A, Ab, A#; B, Bb, Bbb; C, C#, Cb;
D, D#, Db; E, Eb, E#; F#, F♮, Fb.

Key of D:
E, Eb, E#; F#, F♮, Fb; G, G#, Gb;
A, A#, Ab; B, Bb, B#; C#, C♮, Cb.

Lesson 15

The explanatory rules for lesson 14 also apply to lesson 15, 16 and 17.

Key of A:
B, Bb, B#; C#, C♮, Cb; D, D#, Db;
E, E#, Eb; F#, F♮, F×; G#, G♮, Gb.
Key of E:
F#, F♮, F×; G#, G♮, Gb; A, A#, Ab;
B, B#, Bb; C#, C♮, C×; D#, D♮, Db.
Key of B:
C#, C♮, C×; D#, D♮, Db; E, E#, Eb;
F#, F×, F♮; G#, G♮, G×; A#, A♮, Ab.

Lesson 16

Key of F:
G, Gb, G#; A, Ab, Abb; Bb, B♮, Bbb;
C, C#, Cb; D, Db, D#; E, Eb, Ebb.
Key of Bb:
C, Cb, C#; D, Db, Dbb; Eb, E♮, Ebb;
F, F#, Fb; G, Gb, G#; A, Ab, Abb.
Key of Eb:
F, Fb, F#; G, Gb, Gbb; Ab, A♮, Abb;
Bb, B♮, Bbb; C, Cb, C#; D, Db, Dbb.

Lesson 17

Key of Ab:
Bb, Bbb, B♮; C, Cb, Cbb; Db, D♮, Dbb;
Eb, E♮, Ebb; F, Fb, F#; G, Gb, Gbb.
Key of Db:
Eb, Ebb, E♮; F, Fb, Fbb; Gb, G♮, Gbb;
Ab, A♮, Abb; Bb, Bbb, B♮; C, Cb, Cbb.
Key of Gb:
Ab, Abb, A♮; Bb, Bbb, Bbbb; Cb, C♮, Cbb;
Db, D♮, Dbb; Eb, Ebb, E♮; F, Fb, Fbb.

Lesson 18

Line One: M2, 5+, m7, 3°, M6.
Line Two: 4°, m7, 5°, M2, 6+, P4, M7, m2, 4+, M3.
Line Three: 5°, m2, 7°, 5+, M3, M7, m2, 5+, 6+, M3.
Line Four: m6, m3, P4, 6+, 2+, m7, 5°, M3, 2+, P5.
Line Five: 4°, 3°, 4+, m6, 7°, 5+, 2+, m7, M6, m3.
Line Six: 3°, P5, m6, 4°, 2+, 7°, M6, m3, 7°, m6.

Lesson 19

Line One: 2, 7, GF; 4, 5, GD; 3, 6, BG;
5, 4, CF; 7, 2, CD.
Line Two: 6, 3, GB; 5, 4, GC; 3, 6, CA;
4, 5, AE; 7, 2, EF; 2, 7, ED.
Line Three: 2, 7, DC; 4, 5, EB; 6, 3, EG;
7, 2, GA; 3, 6, EC; 5, 4, DG.
Line Fcur: 5, 4, BE; 7, 2, FG; 2, 7, AG;
6, 3, BD; 4, 5, BF; 3, 6, DB.
Line Five: 4, 5, DA; 3, 6, FD; 5, 4, FB;
2, 7, FE; 6, 3, AC; 6, 3, DF.
Line Six: 7, 2, BC; 6, 3, CE; 7, 2, AB;
5, 4, AD; 2, 7, CB; 4, 5, FC.

Lesson 20

Line One: m2, m6, m7, M3, M6, M2, m3.
Line Two: M3, P4, M7, m6, m3, m2, P5, M2, 4+, 5°.
Line Three: 4+, 2+, P5, M7, 4°, m3, 5+, m6, m2, M3.
Line Four: M3, P4, 5+, 3°, 6+, 7°, M2, P4, M6, 5°.
Line Five: 7°, 5+, 3°, 2+, 4°, P5, 6+, M7, m2, P4.
Line Six: 5°, m6, M2, m7, 4+, m3, P5, 3°, M6, 4°.